This Little Explore book belongs to:

MW00892485

_____

For
Curious Learners

© 2022 Grant Publishing

All rights reserved. No part of this publication may be reproduced, distributed or transmitted in any form or means without prior permission of the publisher.

Published by Grant Publishing

Sales and Enquires: grantpublishingltd@gmail.com

FOLLOW US ON SOCIAL MEDIA

 **@grantpublishingltd**

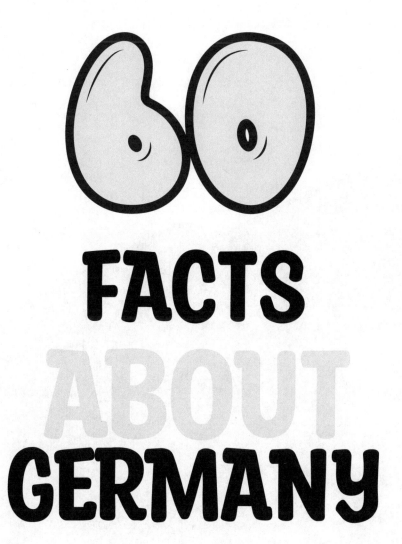

FACTS ABOUT GERMANY

60 Facts About Germany

Hallo, little explorers! Do you love learning about faraway places and cool facts? Well, have you heard about a land full of fairy-tale castles, delicious sausages, and famous inventors? It's called Germany, and it's one of the most fascinating countries in the world!

In this exciting book, you'll dive into the enchanting world of Germany. Prepare to be amazed by fascinating facts that will make your mind soar and vibrant photographs that will transport you to the heart of Germany's vibrant culture. So, get ready to take a journey to Germany through the pages of this book!

For Parents

We know that reading a book about a new country can be an exciting adventure for your child. It's important to remember that kids need breaks, and may not want to read the book all in one sitting. Encourage them to take breaks as needed, and ask them questions about what they've learned so far. Discussing the facts with your child can help them remember and retain the information better. You can also use the book as a springboard for further exploration and learning about Germany. Perhaps you can plan a family outing to try some German food or visit a local museum with exhibits on German culture. Above all, we hope that this book sparks your child's curiosity and inspires them to learn more about the world around them.

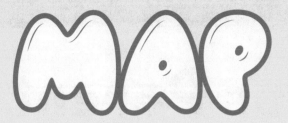

The Facts

1. Germany is a country in the continent of Europe.

DID YOU KNOW?

2. Germany is located in Central Europe and is bordered by nine countries.

EUROPE IS THE SECOND-SMALLEST CONTINENT IN TERMS OF LAND AREA, COVERING ONLY ABOUT 10.18 MILLION SQUARE KILOMETRES, WHICH IS ROUGHLY 2% OF THE EARTH'S SURFACE. DESPITE ITS SMALL SIZE, EUROPE IS THE THIRD-MOST POPULOUS CONTINENT

3. The official name of Germany is the Federal Republic of Germany.

4. Berlin is the capital city of Germany.

HOW MANY CAPTITAL CITIES CAN YOU THINK OF?

Pictured Weingerode, Germany

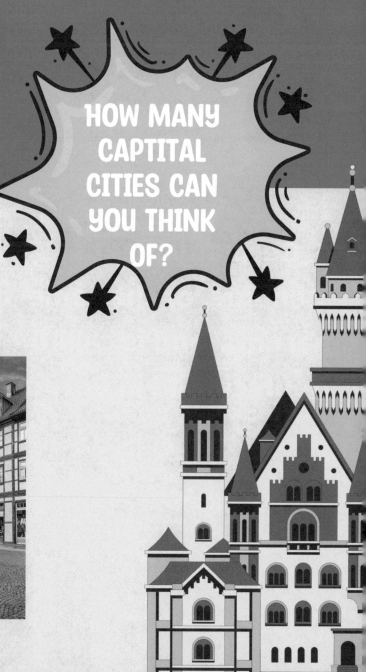

DID YOU KNOW?

Germany is known for its high-quality engineering and is home to several famous car manufacturers like BMW, Volkswagen, and Mercedes-Benz.

5. Berlin is the largest city of Germany.

6. Germany means 'genuine, of the same parents' and is called Deutschland in German.

Pictured Brandenburg, Germany

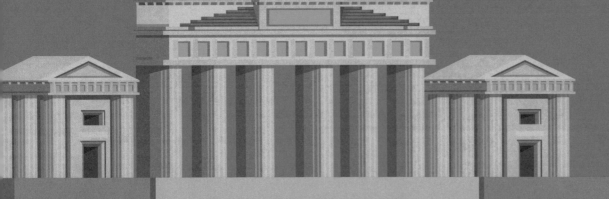

7. Germany is bordered by Denmark, Poland, Czech Republic, Austria, Switzerland, France, Luxembourg, Belgium and the Netherlands.

Pictured Rostock, Germany

8. The official language of Germany is German.

Sound out these phrases

Guten Morgen! (Good morning!)
"goo-ten mor-gen"
Wie geht es Ihnen? (How are you?)
- "vee geht ess ee-nen"

9. Germany is located between the Baltic and North Seas and the Alps.

Germans are known for their love of nature and environmental consciousness.

10. Germany has a population of over 83 million people.

11. Germany is a member state of the European Union.

The European Union (EU) is a political and economic union of 27 member states located in Europe. The EU was established by the Treaty of Maastricht in 1993 with the goal of promoting peace, stability, and economic prosperity in Europe.

12. Germany is the second-most populous country in Europe after Russia.

13. Germany is one of the most densely populated countries in the world.

14. Germany is home to the largest population of Turkish people outside of Turkey.

15. Germany is the fourth-largest economy in the world.

16. The currency is the Euro.

17. The German flag consists of three horizontal stripes: black, red, and gold.

18. People from Germany are called German.

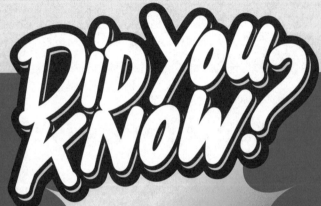

Germany is home to numerous castles, including the famous Neuschwanstein Castle and Heidelberg Castle.

19. Germany is 357,022 square kilometres.

Pictured Dresden, Germany

Dresden is the capital city of the state of Saxony in eastern Germany. It is renowned for its rich history, stunning architecture, and cultural treasures.

20. Germans have a strong tradition of recycling, and the country has one of the most efficient recycling systems in the world.

21. The national anthem is 'Deutschlandlied'

22. Germany is well known for its festival traditions such as Oktoberfest and Christmas.

Oktoberfest is an annual beer festival held in Munich, Germany, and is one of the most famous and largest festivals in the world.

23. Oktoberfest attracts millions of visitors from around the world every year. It is estimated that over 6 million liters of beer are consumed during the festival.

24. Adolf Hitler and his Nazi Party came to power in 1933.

Pictured Adolf Hitler

25. Germany lost World War I to Britain, France, Russia, Italy, Romania, Japan and later the United States.

26. Christianity is the largest religion in Germany.

Pictured Cathedral in Dresden

Germany has had several capital cities. In 1815, Frankfurt-am-Main became the unofficial capital of the German Confederation. In 1871, Berlin was named as the first official capital.

27. Germany has a rich literary history, with famous authors such as Johann Wolfgang von Goethe, Thomas Mann, and Hermann Hesse.

Pictured Johann Wolfgang von Goethe

Johann Wolfgang von Goethe (1749-1832) was a German writer, poet, and philosopher who is considered one of the greatest figures in world literature.

28. Germany is nicknamed 'the land of poets and thinkers'.

29. The Cologne Cathedral is one of the most famous landmarks in Germany and took over 600 years to complete.

Pictured Cologne Cathedral

30. The Rhine River, which flows through Germany, is one of the longest and busiest waterways in Europe.

Pictured The Rhine River

31. Germany is known for its Christmas markets, where people can enjoy festive food, drinks, and shopping.

32. Germany has a strong tradition of classical music, and composers such as Ludwig van Beethoven and Johann Sebastian Bach were born there.

33. Football is the most popular sport in Germany.

34. German scientists have made significant contributions to various fields, including physics, chemistry, and medicine.

DID YOU KNOW?

The national team has won the FIFA World Cup four times.

Pictured Robert Wilhelm and Otto Struve

35. Over 100 Germans have been awarded the Nobel Prize including Albert Einstein who was born in Germany.

Albert Einstein (1879-1955) was a renowned physicist who revolutionized our understanding of the universe.

36. Germany is one of the largest car producers in the world.

37. Germany is the home of famous highway 'the autobahn'.

38. Germany has the most zoos in the world.

ZOO

39. Germany is the second most popular country for migration in the world.

DID YOU KNOW?

In Germany, the working week includes Saturday.

40. Germany is one of the most visited country in the world.

41. One of Germany's most popular tourists attraction is the Miniatur Wunderland, the world's largest model railway.

42. Germany has a temperate climate.

43. In general, Germany has warm summers and cold winters.

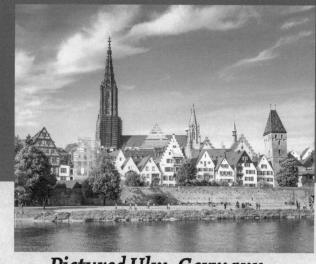

Pictured Ulm, Germany

44. Germany is home to a diverse range of wildlife, including a variety of mammals, birds, reptiles, and marine animals.

45. Germany's largest wooded area is the Black Forest.

46. Germany's thick forests are home to lots of amazing wildlife including wildcats, boars, ibex and the Eurasian Lynx.

47. The highest mountain in Germany is the Zugspitze.

48. Germany contains natural resources such as copper, nickel, natural gas, uranium and coal.

49. Most German dishes contain meat or fish.

50. German cuisine is diverse and includes dishes such as bratwurst, sauerkraut, pretzels, and schnitzel.

51. Germany has a strong tradition of outdoor activities, and hiking and cycling are popular pastimes, with many well-marked trails throughout the country.

52. Germans take pride in their precision and attention to detail, which is reflected in their world-renowned craftsmanship and engineering.

Words that derived from Germany

- Kindergarten
- Doppelgänger
- Wanderlust
- Pretzel
- Rucksack
- Zeitgeist
- Schadenfreude

53. Germany is known for its love of sausages, with hundreds of different varieties available.

54. The German education system is highly regarded, and many universities offer tuition-free education for both domestic and international students.

55. Germany has a rich cultural heritage, with numerous museums, art galleries, and theatres.

YOU CAN DO IT

How many flags can you recognise?

56. The Volkswagen Beetle, created by Ferdinand Porsche, was one of the most iconic cars produced in Germany.

57. The Grimm Brothers, Jacob and Wilhelm, collected and published famous fairy tales such as Cinderella, Sleeping Beauty, and Snow White.

58. Germany has a well-developed public transportation system, including trains, trams, and buses.

59. The Berlin Philharmonic Orchestra is one of the most prestigious orchestras in the world.

The Berlin Philharmonic is composed of highly skilled and talented musicians from around the world.

60. Germany is known for its Christmas traditions, including the Advent wreath, gingerbread cookies, and the Christmas pyramid.

Places To Go

Places To Go

Get ready for an incredible journey to Germany! Grab your backpack, put on your explorer hat, and let's uncover the wonders of this remarkable country. We'll visit fairytale castles, explore vibrant cities, and immerse ourselves in the rich history and culture. From the enchanting Black Forest to the bustling streets of Berlin, each destination will bring new adventures and discoveries. So, buckle up and get ready to make memories that will last a lifetime as we embark on an extraordinary adventure through the heart of Germany!

Berlin: The vibrant capital city of Germany, known for its rich history, world-class museums, and iconic landmarks like the Brandenburg Gate and the Berlin Wall.

Neuschwanstein Castle: Located in Bavaria, this fairy-tale-like castle is a must-visit. Its picturesque setting and enchanting architecture inspired Disney's Sleeping Beauty Castle.

The Black Forest: A stunning region known for its dense forests, charming villages, and scenic hiking trails. Discover the famous cuckoo clocks, enjoy delicious Black Forest cake, and immerse yourself in nature.

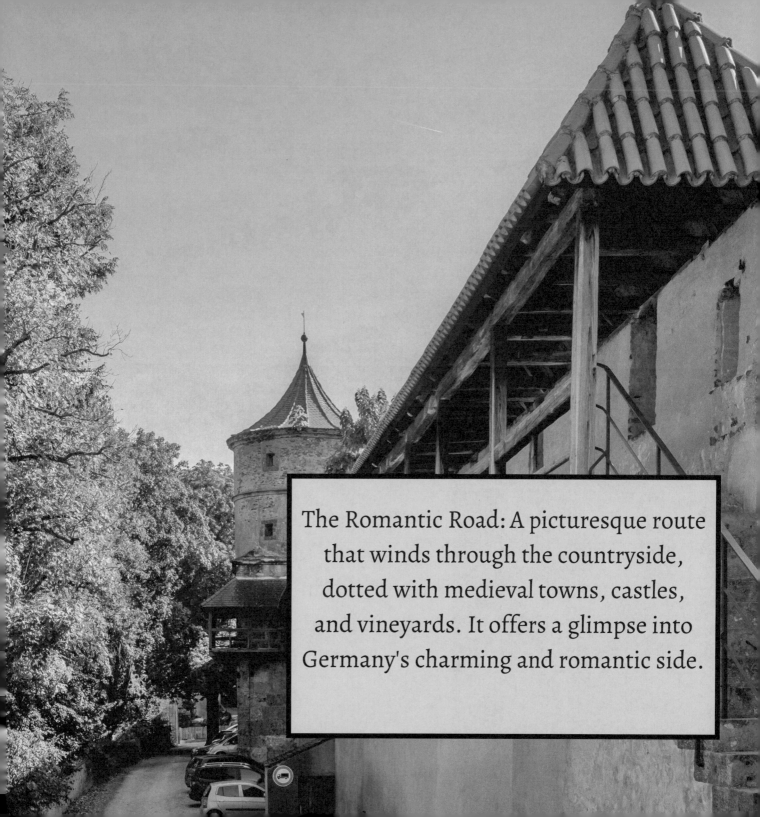

The Romantic Road: A picturesque route that winds through the countryside, dotted with medieval towns, castles, and vineyards. It offers a glimpse into Germany's charming and romantic side.

The Rhine Valley: A breath-taking region along the Rhine River, showcasing beautiful vineyards, charming towns, and stunning castles. Take a scenic boat ride and explore the romantic atmosphere.

Heidelberg: Known for its picturesque old town and the famous Heidelberg Castle, this city offers a blend of history, culture, and stunning views of the Neckar River.

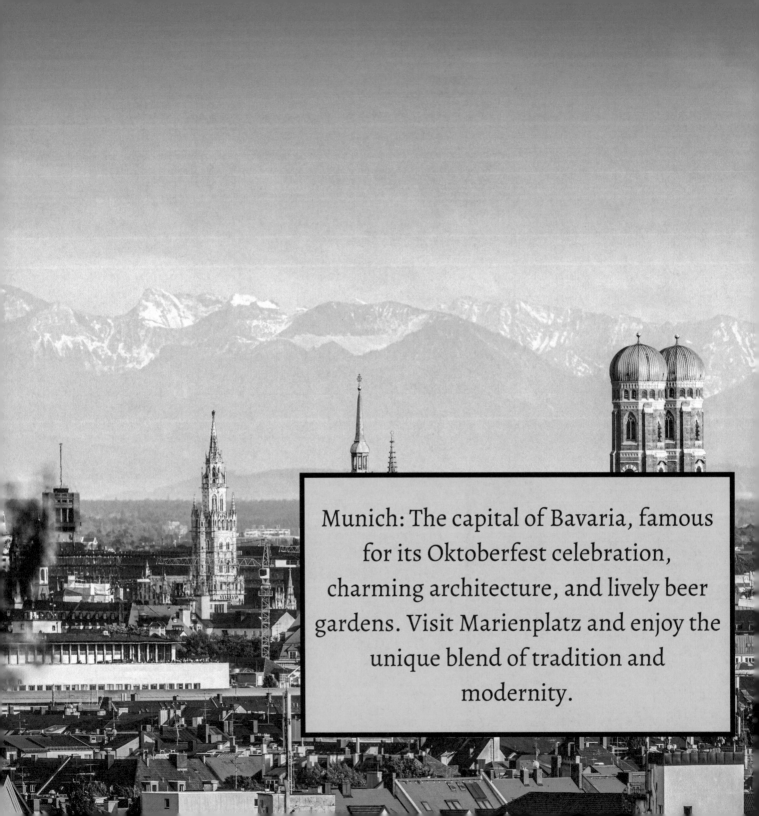

Munich: The capital of Bavaria, famous for its Oktoberfest celebration, charming architecture, and lively beer gardens. Visit Marienplatz and enjoy the unique blend of tradition and modernity.

Dresden: A city renowned for its stunning Baroque architecture, including the impressive Dresden Frauenkirche and the Zwinger Palace. Explore its rich cultural heritage and visit world-class museums.

The Baltic Sea Coast: Discover the beautiful sandy beaches, picturesque coastal towns, and unique landscapes along Germany's Baltic Sea coastline. Enjoy the refreshing sea breeze and soak up the maritime charm.

Zugspitze: As the highest peak in Germany, Zugspitze offers breathtaking panoramic views of the surrounding Alps. You can take a cable car or cogwheel train to reach the summit and enjoy activities like skiing, hiking, and even visiting an ice palace.`

The Moselle Valley: Known for its picturesque vineyards, the Moselle Valley is a wine lover's paradise. Explore the charming towns along the Moselle River, visit local wineries, and savor the delicious wines produced in the region.

The Bavarian Alps: If you're a fan of outdoor adventures, the Bavarian Alps are perfect for you. Experience stunning mountain landscapes.

Sanssouci Palace: Located in Potsdam, near Berlin, Sanssouci Palace is a magnificent rococo palace surrounded by beautifully landscaped gardens.

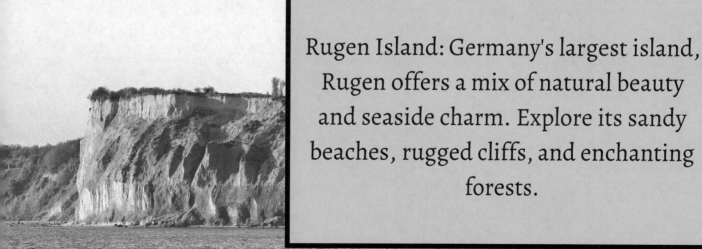

Rugen Island: Germany's largest island, Rugen offers a mix of natural beauty and seaside charm. Explore its sandy beaches, rugged cliffs, and enchanting forests.

Explore

Explore

Welcome to the "Explore" section! It's time to put your knowledge of Germany to the test with some exciting trivia questions. Challenge yourself and see how much you know about Germany's fascinating history, famous landmarks, and cultural traditions. Don't worry if you don't know all the answers, this is a great opportunity to learn and discover more about this amazing country. So, grab a pen and paper, gather your friends and family, and let the Germany trivia adventure begin!

Test Yourself

Q: What is Germany?

A: Germany is a country located in Europe.

Q: What is the capital city of Germany?

A: The capital city of Germany is Berlin.

Q: What language do people speak in Germany?

A: The main language spoken in Germany is German.

Q: What is a famous German landmark that looks like a castle?

A: Neuschwanstein Castle is a famous castle in Germany.

Q: What is a traditional German food that looks like a giant pretzel?

A: A traditional German food that looks like a giant pretzel is called a Brezel.

Test Yourself

Q: What are some famous German cars?

A: Some famous German car brands are Volkswagen, BMW, and Mercedes-Benz.

Q: What is a popular German festival where people wear traditional clothes and dance?

A: The Oktoberfest festival is a popular German festival where people wear traditional clothes and dance.

Q: Which famous fairy tale characters were born from German stories?

A: Fairy tale characters like Cinderella, Snow White, and Hansel and Gretel originated from German stories.

Q: What animal is often associated with Germany?

A: The eagle is often associated with Germany and can be seen on the German coat of arms.

Activities To Try

Activities

Welcome to the Activities section! Get ready for exciting adventures exploring Germany. In this section, you'll discover a wide range of fun and interactive activities that will help you dive into German culture and history. From crafting your own German castle to tasting delicious German treats, and even learning some traditional German dances, there's something for everyone. Feel free to put your own twist on these activities and let your imagination soar! So, buckle up and get ready to have a blast while discovering all the wonders of Germany in a whole new way!

Design Your Own Pretzel

Materials needed:

Paper

Coloured pencils or markers

Instructions:

1. Discuss with children about pretzels, a popular snack in Germany.
2. Instruct them to draw and design their own pretzel shapes on the paper using the colored pencils or markers.
3. Encourage creativity and variety with colors and decorations.
4. Once finished, have the children share their pretzel designs and discuss what inspired their choices.

Create a German Flag Collage

Materials needed:

Construction paper (black, red, and yellow)

Glue

Scissors

Instructions:

1. Show children the German flag and explain its colors and meaning.
2. Provide them with construction paper in black, red, and yellow.
3. Instruct them to cut out rectangles of the correct proportions from each color.
4. Help them glue the rectangles onto a larger piece of paper in the correct order to create the German flag.
5. Allow them to be creative by adding additional elements or drawings to their flag collages.

Learn a German Song

Materials needed:

Song lyrics or printouts of a German children's song

Instructions:

1. Introduce children to a popular German children's song.
2. Provide them with the lyrics or printouts of the song.
3. Play the song and encourage children to listen and follow along with the lyrics.
4. Teach them the melody and words, and practice singing the song together.

Build a Miniature Neuschwanstein Castle

Materials needed:

Craft materials (cardboard, paper, glue, scissors, markers)

Optional: Popsicle sticks, paint

Instructions:

1. Show children pictures of Neuschwanstein Castle and discuss its unique features.
2. Provide them with craft materials to build a miniature version of the castle.
3. Instruct them to use cardboard for the main structure, paper for details, and popsicle sticks for support if desired.
4. Encourage creativity by coloring or painting the castle and adding any additional decorations.
5. Once complete, children can proudly display their miniature Neuschwanstein Castle.

Make German Paper Lanterns

Materials needed:

Coloured paper

Scissors

Glue

Markers

Optional: String or pipe cleaners

Instructions:

1. Show children examples of German paper lanterns and discuss their significance.
2. Provide them with coloured paper, scissors, and glue.
3. Instruct them to cut out strips or shapes from the paper to create the lantern.
4. Show them how to fold and glue the paper to form the lantern shape.
5. Encourage creativity by using markers to add designs or patterns to the lantern.
6. Optional: Attach string or pipe cleaners to create handles for the lanterns.
7. Once finished, children can light up their lanterns using battery-operated candles or glow sticks.

Glossary

Glossary

Germany: A country located in Europe known for its rich history, culture, and beautiful landscapes.

Berlin: The capital city of Germany, known for its famous landmarks like the Brandenburg Gate and the Berlin Wall.

Oktoberfest: A famous German festival held annually in Munich, known for its lively atmosphere, traditional music, and delicious food.

Neuschwanstein Castle: A stunning castle located in Bavaria, Germany, known for its fairy-tale-like appearance and being an inspiration for Disney's Sleeping Beauty Castle.

Volkswagen: A famous German car manufacturer known for producing popular car models such as the Beetle and the Golf.

Autobahn: The German highway system famous for its sections without speed limits, where cars can drive at high speeds.

Brezel: A traditional German pretzel, a popular snack made from twisted dough and sprinkled with coarse salt.

Black Forest: A beautiful region in southwestern Germany known for its dense forests, cuckoo clocks, and the famous Black Forest cake.

Fairy Tales: Germany is the birthplace of many beloved fairy tales, including Snow White, Cinderella, and Hansel and Gretel, written by the Brothers Grimm.

Rhine River: One of the longest rivers in Europe, flowing through Germany, known for its scenic landscapes, historic castles, and vineyards.

Author's Note

Dear young readers,

I am so excited to have shared with you all about Germany, a country that is rich in history, art and culture. As an author, I am always inspired by the incredible diversity and beauty of the world around us, and I hope this book has inspired you to explore and learn more about Germany.

I was inspired to write this book because I believe that learning about different cultures and countries can help us understand and appreciate the world better. It's so important to celebrate and learn from different traditions and ways of life, and I hope this book has helped you do just that.

If you enjoyed reading this book, I would love it if you could leave a review on Amazon. Reviews help other readers discover the book and can make a big difference for independent authors like myself.
Thank you for joining me on this journey, and I hope this book has sparked your curiosity and imagination. Keep exploring and learning about the world around you!

Sincerely,
Grant Publishing

Made in the USA
Columbia, SC
31 August 2024

41358444R10041